ॐ

The

SANSKRIT ALPHABET

Ashwini Kumar Aggarwal

जय गुरुदेव

ॐ

ISBN13: 978-93-5268-659-9 Paperback Edition
ISBN13: 978-93-48012-27-2 Hardbound Edition
Digital Edition also available

Title: **The Sanskrit Alphabet**
Author: **Ashwini Kumar Aggarwal**

4th May 2017 Thursday, Sita Navami
Vaisakha Masa, Shukla Paksha, Uttarayana
Saka Samvat 1939 Hemalambi, Vikram Samvat 2074 Sadharana

Devotees of Sri Sri Ravi Shankar Ashram

The Art of Living Centre
147 Punjabi Bagh, Patiala 147001
Punjab, India

Website advaita56.weebly.com

1st Edition May 2017

जय गुरुदेव

ॐ

Dedication

Gurudev Sri Sri Ravi Shankar

Our path giver

An offering at His Lotus feet

जय गुरुदेव

Preface

This book arose out of the adventures faced in typing Sanskrit on the computer.

When we used to write Sanskrit in school then it was quite easy as we could form any letter of our choice as per need in constructing a sentence.

However the challenge surfaced when interest arose in putting the knowledge gained into print. Most word processors either lacked the font glyphs or it was difficult to ascertain how to correctly type a particular character.

Since the scriptures were handed down in an oral tradition, most of the sounds were never written but only spoken! The system of writing developed rather recently and is still undergoing change. There are variations in notations, character usage and spelling in the various printed texts.

In English texts, there is always a tendency to spell a Sanskrit word without the ending visarga or the makara, or in its stem form. Here also a strict Sanskrit spelling in first case प्रथमा विभक्ति or in बहुवचन has not been adhered to, to keep the text light and lively.

A reasonable level of fluency having been attained in Sanskrit, this book has been written to share the knowledge for common benefit.

Foreword

संस्कृत को देवों की भाषा कहा गया। संस्कृत में ही वेदों का बखान हुआ। उपनिषद का उल्लेख हो, या कालिदास की 'उट्र से लेकर उष्ट्र' तक की यात्रा, महाभारत का हृदय विदारक वर्णन हो या गीता का ज्ञान, गुरु–शिष्य की गूढ़ वार्ता हो या माँ दुर्गा की स्तुति, संस्कृत के बिना तो कुछ भी अभिव्यक्त न हुआ।

आदिकाल में एकमात्र संस्कृत भाषा का ही आधिपत्य था, जिसने प्रत्येक कवि, लेखक, साहित्यकार, शैलीकार या कहानीकार की लेखनी से न केवल अभिव्यक्ति पाई, वरन उससे असीम सफलता भी पाई। आधुनिक युग की भी हर भाषा व लिपि का मूल संस्कृत में ही तो है।
Australia originated from 'अष्ट्र + आलय', the twelve months January to December find their roots and meaning in Sanskrit.

आज के वैज्ञानिकों ने भी अपनी शोध (research) के द्वारा संस्कृत के उच्चारण व पठन–पाठन से मन मस्तिष्क पर पड़ने वाले सकारात्म प्रभावों को देखा, परखा और अनुमोदित (recommend) किया है। इसीलिए मात्र भारतवर्ष ही नहीं अपितु भौतिक साधनों में अगृणी पाश्चात्य देशों में भी संस्कृत की शिक्षा–दीक्षा को प्राथमिक शिक्षा स्तर पर ही अनिवार्य करने की जागरूकता आई है।

'The Sanskrit Alphabet' is one of the most basic, essential yet most profound work in the direction of making Sanskrit learning, reading, writing, and typing with keyboard, not only possible but effective and efficient.

इस मूलभूत प्रयास से आज की पीढ़ी भी आसानी से जान सकेगी संस्कृत को। यह प्रयास एक कड़ी की भांति जोड़ सकेगा आधुनिक पीढ़ी को वैदिक ज्ञान–कोष की जड़ो से, और सशक्त सांस्कृतिक धरोहरों से, वह भी समकालीन प्रौद्योगिकी व तकनीकी ज्ञान के साथ साथ।

मैं हृदय से आभार व्यक्त करती हूँ और साधुवाद देती हूँ श्रीमान अश्विनी अग्रवाल जी को, इस सोच के लिए तथा उन अथक प्रयासों के लिए जिनके फलस्वरूप यह पुस्तक इस मूर्त रूप में आई। बधाई अर्पित है प्रेरणास्रोत, ज्ञान मूर्ति गुरुदेव के चरण कमलों में।

इस पुस्तक में अनिवार्य ज्ञान को सरल, क्रमबद्ध व सुनियोजित प्रकार से इस भांति लिखा गया है कि हर स्तर के (प्रारम्भिक, नौसिखिए, या विशेषज्ञ) पाठकों को अनिवार्य मार्गदर्शन के साथ साथ प्रेरणा भी मिलेगी।

शुभेच्छाओं के साथ

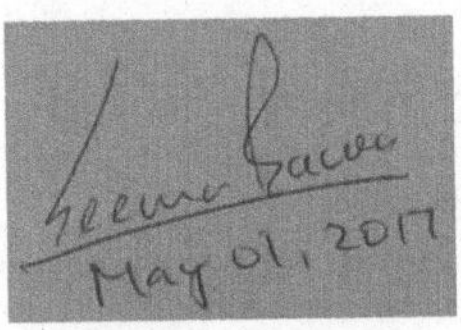

(Dr. Seema Bawa)
Professor, Comp. Sc. & Engg.
Ex–Dean (Student Affairs)
Ex–Head (Comp. Sc. & Engg.)
Professor In-Charge Nava Nalanda Central Library
Thapar University, Patiala

Table of Contents

Blessing

Let us do the आ Meditation. Notice that as you chant mentally, the sound never dies. You can chant eternally. The Sanskrit word for alphabet is अक्षर । न क्षरति इति अक्षर । That which has no decay is called the Alphabet.

H H Sri Sri Ravi Shankar
5th February 2017, Gita Ek Samvaad, New Delhi

Introduction

The Sanskrit Alphabet वर्णमाला consists of 56 letters.
vowels स्वर - 20 (popular tradition lists 13, without pluta vowels)
consonants व्यञ्जन - 34 (popular tradition lists 33, without ळ)
anusvara and visarga – 2 (there are 4 additional vedic ayogavahas)

> a written consonant क is usually supplied with the vowel अ for purpose of enunciation. Without a vowel, the हलन्त symbol is used to write a consonant. Actual consonant should be with a halant e.g. क् । Such a consonant is technically termed a half-letter.

the ह् is an aspirate, i.e. mahaprana. it is named thus.
the hakara is also an exception when writing conjuncts. संयुक्त अक्षर

Anusvara and Candrabindu
An anusvara ं is a nasal नासिका । uttered with mouth closed and emphasis on the nose. usually pronounced as म्
The candrabindu ँ is an anunasika अनुनासिका । uttered from the mouth with emphasis on the nose. pronounced as न् or म्

the jihvamuliya ᳵ is a guttural visarga

the upadhmaniya ᳶ or ᳶ is a labial visarga

Avagraha ऽ denotes the elision of अ आ to prevent loss of meaning.
ळ is usually found in Vedic texts and rarely in classical sanskrit.

Sanskrit numerals combine like the English numerals in number representation, viz. units, decimals, thousands, etc.

This work is relevant both for the western reader as well as the Indian audience. So the usage of diacritics is kept to a minimum. Enjoy exploring the letters and sounds that have found a place in all the languages of the world.

The Sanskrit Alphabet

संस्कृत वर्णमाला

अ आ इ ई उ ऊ ऋ ॠ ऌ ॡ   ए ऐ ओ औ   अं अः   अँ

क्	ख्	ग्	घ्	ङ्	The Shiva Sounds
च्	छ्	ज्	झ्	ञ्	
ट्	ठ्	ड्	ढ्	ण्	The Brahma Sounds
त्	थ्	द्	ध्	न्	
प्	फ्	ब्	भ्	म्	The Vishnu Sounds
य् र् ल् व्		श् ष् स्		ह्	
		ळ्	ळ्ह्		Vedic Sanskrit
० १ २ ३ ४ ५ ६ ७ ८ ९					Numerals
क्ष ज्ञ श्र					Conjunct letter

Additional letters found in Vedic Sanskrit are ळ and ळ्ह् ।

The consonant ळ is an alternate version of ड् alpaprana usage.

अग्निमीडे → अग्निमीळे agnimīḍe → agnimīḻe

अग्निम् ईडे Agni (is to be) praised. ई ड् ए → ई ळ् ए Rigveda 1.1.1

Likewise ळ्ह् replaces ढ् in mahaprana usage.

दृढं → दृळ्हं dṛḍhaṁ → dṛḻhaṁ दृ ढ् अं → दृ ळ्ह् अं Rigveda 4.1.1

The vowel long ॡ is not found in literature. It is given only in the alphabet, grammar books or in font sets. Hence crossed out.

Font glyph variations in some old Sanskrit texts

अ अ , आ आ , ओ ओ , औ औ , झ झ , ण ण

Conjunct letter संयुक्त अक्षर

क्ष ज्ञ श्र are not letters of the alphabet. Rather these are conjuncts that have become popular in writing. An earlier form of क्ष is क्ष ।

Characteristics of Letters

In the Sanskrit Alphabet, the letters have distinct characteristics.

Simple Vowels - अ आ इ ई उ ऊ ऋ ॠ ऌ

Short Vowels ह्रस्व - अ इ उ ऋ ऌ called लघु स्वर light syllable
Long Vowels दीर्घ - आ ई ऊ ॠ
Conjunct Vowels - ऋ (अर्) ॠ (आर्) ऌ (अल्)

Diphthong Vowels - ए ऐ ओ औ

Vowel compounds - ए (अ इ) ऐ (आ इ) ओ (अ उ) औ (आ उ)
Also known as गुरु स्वर heavy syllable

Ayogavaha अयोगवाह Sounds - अनुस्वार अं , विसर्जनीय अः , चंद्रबिंदु अँ

Row class consonants
क् ख् ग् घ् ङ्   च् छ् ज् झ् ञ्   ट् ठ् ड् ढ् ण्   त् थ् द् ध् न्   प् फ् ब् भ् म्

Semivowels अन्तःस्थ midway between vowel and consonant य् र् ल् व्

Sibilants ऊष्म - श् ष् स्

Aspirate ऊष्म तथा महाप्राण – ह्

Vedic Sandhi letters ळ् ळ्ह्

Vedic Ayogavaha Sounds अᳵ, अᳶ, ꣳ(गुँ , गं्), ꣴ, हुँ, र्, ष
Numerals are combined just as in English to form succeeding numbers, e.g. १० ११ १२ ५०१ ८५६७

Alphabet as Commonly Written

The Sanskrit alphabet is commonly written without a halant. Consonants cannot be uttered without a vowel. So in teaching, each consonant is supplied with the vowel अ , so that it can be uttered. Here are the 56 letters of the classical Sanskrit Alphabet.

20 Vowels

अ आ अ३ इ ई इ३ उ ऊ उ३ ऋ ॠ ऋ३ ऌ ऌ३ ए ऐ ए३ ओ औ ओ३

34 Consonants

क ख ग घ ङ

च छ ज झ ञ

ट ठ ड ढ ण

त थ द ध न

प फ ब भ म

य र ल व

श ष स ह

ळ

2 Ayogavahas

अं अः

Vowels

अ आ इ ई उ ऊ ऋ ॠ ऌ ए ऐ ओ औ अं अः

Consonants

क	ख	ग	घ	ङ
च	छ	ज	झ	ञ
ट	ठ	ड	ढ	ण
त	थ	द	ध	न
प	फ	ब	भ	म

य र ल व

श ष स ह

Grammar schools usually teach it like this.

Unicodes for Letters

The Unicode consortium has fixed the alphanumeric hex codes so that there is uniformity across devices and operating systems in typing the letters. For Devanagari script letters, the unicodes go from 0900 to 097F. Rather easy to remember because India's country code for international phone dialling is +91.

In case one has forgotten hex coding, no matter. Decimal numbers go from 0 to 9, i.e. ten digits, and then combine to make 10, 11 etc. Similarly hex numbers go from 0 to 9 then A B C D E F, i.e. 16 digits, then combine to make 10, 11, 12, 13, 14, 15, 16, 17, 18, 19, 1A, 1B, 1C, 1D, 1E, 1F, 20, 21, etc.

The online charts for Unicodes are available at
http://www.unicode.org/charts/#scripts
The unicodes relevant for Sanskrit are in the three different charts named Devanagari, Devanagari Extended and Vedic Extensions.

More resources
http://www.unicode.org/faq/indic.html
http://www.unicode.org/resources/keyboards.html
http://www.unicode.org/resources/fonts.html
http://www.unicode.org/resources/online-tools.html

अ0905 आ0906 etc. These letters are easy to enter on a computer. However we may find it difficult to type the special letters, so some of these are listed. To type any of these characters, simply enter the unicode and then press **ALT+x** keys on a windows computer.

E.g. to type ॐ, type 0950 **ALT+x** and the symbol ॐ appears, if the relevant font is installed in your machine.

अँ 0901	ळ 0933	ऽ 093D	ॠ 0908	ॠ 0960	ऌ 090C	◌् 094D
ॐ 0950	◌ॎ 094E	॰ 0970	◌ृ 0943	◌ॄ 0944	◌ॢ 0962	0971
◌़ 093C	ड़ 095C	ढ़ 095D	ज़ 095B	॑ 0951	॒ 0952	᳚ 1CDA
। 0964	॥ 0965	ॺ 097A	ᳲ 1CF2	A8F2	ꣳ A8F3	ꣴ A8F4
᳭ 1CED	ᳶ 1CF6	᳙ 1CD9	◌ॖ 0956		₹ 20B9	√ 221A

General paper on Indic scripts
https://www.w3.org/2002/Talks/09-ri-indic/indic-paper.html

Standard fonts
https://www.google.com/get/noto/
Writing
https://www.linotype.com/6896/devanagari.html

Legacy font for typing Half Letters

ट ह् ज् ९ न् म् ह

http://indiatyping.com/index.php/download/201-shusha-font

Font for typing most Devanagari Vedic letters, Ligatures and Glyphs

त्र F100 द्व F106 भ्क F107 ग्ग F10A ॐ F15A ं F141 F306

http://svayambhava.blogspot.in/p/siddhanta-devanagariunicode-open-type.html
https://omkarananda-ashram.org/Sanskrit/itranslator2003.htm

Pluta Vowels

In the Vedic texts, pluta vowels are encountered that are rare in classical Sanskrit. Pluta signifies elongation of a vowel while speaking to 3 or more time lengths मात्रा । The English term for प्लुत is prolated or protacted.

Thus we have
अ Time length of one matra in speaking – short vowel ह्रस्व
आ Time length of two matras in speaking – long vowel दीर्घ
अ३ Time length of three matras in speaking – pluta vowel प्लुत
The pluta is written variously – अ३, आ३, आ२ — all meaning the same. A pluta vowel does not combine in sandhi.

This set has 20 letters

अ	आ	अ३
इ	ई	इ३
उ	ऊ	उ३
ऋ	ॠ	ऋ३
ऌ	-	ऌ३
ए	ऐ	ए३
ओ	औ	ओ३

E.g. for pluta vowel from a Rudrashtadhyayi text 2nd adhyaya.

एतावानस्य महिमातोज् ज्यायाँ२ श्च पूरुषः । Purushasuktam

Accented Vowels

अनुदात्त , उदात्त , स्वरित स्वराः

In the Vedic texts, accented vowels are seen. The accent signifies a change in pitch or tone of the vowel. Known as स्वर ।

अ॒ Anudata accent to specify lowering of pitch in speaking - low

अ Udata accent to specify standard pitch in speaking - normal

अ॑ Svarita accent to specify raising of pitch in speaking - high

Additionally, the dirgha svarita (double svarita) accent is also seen.

अ᳚ dirgha Svarita accent to specify raising of pitch for extended time length then lowering to normal – high to normal

> Note - even though the texts mention उदात्त to mean raised***, in actual practise when we do Vedic chanting***, the Udata Svaras (unmarked letters in the text) are chanted in normal tone and Anudatas are clearly lowered while Svaritas are in high pitch.

अ अ॒ अ॑ आ आ॒ आ॑ अ᳚ आ᳚

इ इ॒ इ॑ ई ई॒ ई॑ इ᳚ ई᳚

उ उ॒ उ॑ ऊ ऊ॒ ऊ॑ उ᳚ ऊ᳚

ऋ ऋ॒ ऋ॑ ॠ ॠ॒ ॠ॑

ऌ ऌ॒ ऌ॑

ए ए॒ ए॑ ऐ ऐ॒ ऐ॑ ए᳚ ऐ᳚

ओ ओ॒ ओ॑ औ औ॒ औ॑ ओ᳚ औ᳚

E.g. for accented vowel from a Rudrashtadhyayi text 2nd adhyaya.

ए॒तावा॑नस्य महि॒मातो॒ज् ज्यायाँ᳚ २ श्च॒ पूरु॑षः । Purusha Suktam

E.g. for accented vowel from a Ganapati Atharvashirsha text.

ग॒णादिं᳚ पूर्व॑मुच्चा॒र्य॒ व॒र्णादीं᳚ स्तद॒नन्तरम् । अनुस्वारꣳ प॑रत॒रः । अर्धे᳚न्दुल॒सितम् ।

Nasalized Consonants

The 5th of row class consonants are nasalized, i.e they must be uttered with emphasis on the nose. Thus ङ् ञ् ण् न् म् are pronounced from their respective places as given and also from the nose, hence called Anunasika i.e. Nasalized.

In the Vedic texts, nasalized semivowels are also noticed. Only the three semivowel consonants viz. य् ल् व् can be nasalized in certain situations of Sandhi. These are then written with a candrabindu as यँ्, लँ्, वँ् respectively.

This set has 8 letters

ङ् ञ् ण् न् म्

यँ् लँ् वँ्

E.g. for nasalized semivowel from a Rudram text.

त्र्य॑म्बकयँ॒ यजामहे सुग॒न्धिं पु॒ष्टि॒वर्ध॑नम् ।

E.g. for nasalized semivowel from a Guru Puja text.

तत् पदं दर्शितयँ॒ येन तस्मै श्री गुरवे नमः ।

Nasalization of Vowels

A vowel may be nasalized due to a specific Sandhi situation. Thus अ becomes अँ , आ becomes आँ , इ becomes इँ and so on.

This set has 15 letters

अँ आँ अँ३

इँ ईँ इँ३

उँ ऊँ उँ३

एँ ऐँ एँ३

ओँ औँ ओँ३

Note – The eternal sound Om ओम् = nasalized ओ = ओँ = ॐ

Its enunciation would be Aum or Om or Onkara as per context or tradition.

E.g. for nasalized vowel from a Rudrashtadhyayi text 2nd adhyaya.

ए॒तावा॑नस्य महि॒मातो॒ज्॒ ज्यायाँ॑२श्च॒ पूरु॑षः । Purusha Suktam

E.g. for nasalized vowel from a Rudrashtadhyayi text 5th adhyaya.

अहीँश्च सर्वा॑ञ्ज॒म्भय॑न्त्सर्वा॑श्च यातुधा॒न्यो॑ऽध॒राची॒ः परा॑सुव । Namakam / Shat-Rudriya

E.g. for nasalized vowel from a RigVeda text Mandala 1.4.13.

सुस॑मिद्धो न॒ आव॑ह दे॒वाँ अ॑ग्ने ह॒विष्म॑ते ।

Use of candrabindu is common in Hindi and Marathi literature.

Alphabet table for a Vowel

Vowel अ can take the following 18 forms.

Non-nasalized निर् अनुनासिक Nasalized अनुनासिक

अ	आ	अ३	Regular	अँ	आँ	अँ३
अ	अ॒	अ॑	Accented Short	अँ	अँ॒	अँ॑
आ	आ॒	आ॑	Accented Long	आँ	आँ॒	आँ॑

Note – Regular and Accented seem to have the same forms अ , अँ repeated, however one is a Regular form and the other is an Udata accented form of Vedic Sanskrit.

Vowel अ can take the additional 2 forms of accent dirgha Svarita.

अ᳚ आ᳚

Similarly Vowels इ , उ can take these 18+2=20 forms.

Vowel ऋ can take the 18 forms. Dirgha Svarita not noticed.
Vowel ऌ can take the 12 forms only as long ॡ is not noticed.

Diphthong Vowels ए , ओ have the following 12 forms.

Non-nasalized निर् अनुनासिक Nasalized अनुनासिक

ए	ऐ	ए३	Regular	एँ	ऐँ	एँ३
ए	ए॒	ए॑	Accented	एँ	ऐँ॒	एँ॑

Additional 2 forms of accent dirgha Svarita

ए᳚ ऐ᳚

Maheshwar Sutras

माहेश्वराणि सूत्राणि Encompasses sounds that are the foundation of the Devanagari Alphabet. Attributed to Maharishi Panini circa 600 BC.

1	अ इ उ	ण्	All vowels = अ च् letters
2	ऋ ऌ	क्	Simple vowels = अ क् letters
3	ए ओ	ङ्	Diphthongs = ए च् letters
4	ऐ औ	च्	Semivowels = य ण् letters
Vowel – Consonant boundary			
5	ह य व र	ट्	All consonants = ह ल् letters
6	लँ	ण्	=ल्+अँ, No nasal equiv for र्
7	ञ म ङ ण न	म्	5th of row = Nasals = ञ म् letters
8	झ भ	ञ्	4th of row = झ ष् letters
9	घ ढ ध	ष्	are all soft consonants
10	ज ब ग ड द	श्	3rd of row = ज श् letters (soft)
11	ख फ छ ठ थँ च ट त	व्	1st and 2nd of row = ख य् letters
12	क प	य्	are all hard consonants
13	श ष स	र्	Sibilants (hard) = श र् letters
14	ह	ल्	Aspirate is soft

From these 14 Sutras are cognised the 44 Pratyaharas (Arrays), used in the Ashtadhyayi of Panini, and the precursor for modern day computer programming code.

Pronunciation of Sanskrit Letters

उच्चारण
अ son आ father इ it ई beat उ full ऊ pool ऋ rhythm
ॠ marine ऌ revelry ॡ ए play ऐ aisle ओ go औ loud
अं Anusvara is pure nasal – close the lips – similar to म्
अः Visarga is Breath release like ह् and preceding vowel sound
e.g. Pronounce नमः as नमह , शान्तिः as शान्तिहि , विष्णुः as विष्णुह

क seeK	ख Khan	ग Get	घ loGHut	ङ sing
च Chunk	छ catchhim	ज Jump	झ heDGEhog	ञ bunch
ट True	ठ anTHill	ड Drum	ढ goDHead	ण under
त Tamil	थ Thunder	द That	ध breaTHE	न nut
प Put	फ Fruit	ब Bin	भ abhor	म much

य loYal र Red ल Luck व Vase श Sure ष Shun स So Hum ह

Conjuncts in general – first utter the top part and then the bottom one, e.g.

Bhagavad Gita 10.16 तिष्ठसि → ष् ठ ,

Bhagavad Gita 10.23 शङ्करश्चास्मि → ङ् क , श् च

Specific Conjuncts

ह् ण = ह्ण , ह् न = ह्न , ह् म = ह्म
Utter with emphasis on the chest, first the nasal and then the aspiration, e.g. Brahma = ब्रह्म *Pronounce as* ***Bramha***

Shiksha Vedanga – Science of Pronunciation

Sanskrit is a language that was orally passed on from generation to generation. There are many sections in the Vedic and later texts that talk about the letters of the alphabet and their proper intonation, enunciation and phonetics शिक्षा ।

Taittiriya Upanishad Shiksha Valli
शीक्षां व्याख्यास्यामः । वर्णः स्वरः । मात्रा बलम् । साम सन्तानः ।
इत्युक्तः शीक्षाध्यायः ॥ १.२ (Chapter 1 Anuvaka 2)

Taittiriya Pratisakhya तैत्तिरीय प्रातिशाख्य
अथ वर्णसमाम्नायः ॥ १॥ (Chapter 1)
स्वराः स्पर्शात् तथा अन्तःस्था ऊष्माणः च अथ दर्शिताः ।
विसर्ग_अनुस्वार_ळाः च नासिक्याः पञ्च च उदिताः ॥

Paniniya Shiksha पाणिनीय शिक्षा लघु पाठः / वृद्ध पाठः
आकाशवायुप्रभवः शरीरात् समुच्चरन् वक्त्रमुपैति नादः । १.१

Paniniya Shiksha पाणिनीय शिक्षा श्लोकात्मिका
अथ शिक्षां प्रवक्ष्यामि पाणिनीयं मतं यथा । १.१

The Rigved Pratisakhya ऋग्वेद प्रातिशाख्य and Vajasneyi Pratisakhya वाजसनेयी प्रातिशाख्य are also notable texts on शिक्षा ।

Utter each letter clearly and distinctly, with proper position of the tongue in the mouth. This is the aim of the Shiksha texts. It will take some time to practise and getting used to the correct method of reading a Sanskrit letter and text. However it is most rewarding, as our anatomy, bones and muscles are all connected to sound, the key aspect of the fundamental element space.

Place & Effort of Enunciation

Place of speech	Vowels स्वर		Row Consonants व्यञ्जन Alpaprana Mahaprana					Semi vow el	Sibi lant
	Short	Long	1st	2nd	3rd	4th	5th		
कण्ठ	अ	आ	क	ख	ग	घ	ङ		
तालु	इ	ई	च	छ	ज	झ	ञ	य	श
मूर्धा	ऋ	ॠ	ट	ठ	ड	ढ	ण	र	ष
दन्त	ऌ		त	थ	द	ध	न	ल	स
ओष्ठ	उ	ऊ	प	फ	ब	भ	म		
Consonants are supplied with vowel अ to aid enunciation									

कण्ठ - तालु	ए ऐ	Diphthongs have twin places of utterance, being compound vowels
कण्ठ - ओष्ठ	ओ औ	
दन्त - ओष्ठ	व	The vakara is different from the other semivowels as it has twin places of utterance
नासिक्य	ं , अं	Anusvara is a pure Nasal
अनुनासिका	ँ , ॐ , यँ	Candrabindu means Nasalization

<table>
<tr><td rowspan="2">कण्ठ
Soft, Mahaprana</td><td>ह</td><td>Hakara is an Aspirate. It is sounded like a soft release of breath</td></tr>
<tr><td>◌ः</td><td>Visarga is an Aspirate. It is sounded like ह alongwith its preceding vowel</td></tr>
<tr><td colspan="3">Ardha Visarga ◌ः is also written as ᳵ</td></tr>
<tr><td>Base of tongue
Hard, Alpaprana</td><td>◌ः or ᳵ</td><td>Jihvamuliya pronounce as ह्
(a visarga preceding क , ख)</td></tr>
<tr><td>ओष्ठ
Hard, Alpaprana</td><td>◌ः or ᳵ

or ᳶ</td><td>Upadhmaniya pronounce as फ्
(a visarga preceding प , फ)</td></tr>
</table>

कण्ठ्य Guttural or Velar	तालव्य Palatal	मूर्धन्य Cerebral or Retroflex or Lingual	दन्त्य Dental	ओष्ठ्य Labial

All vowels and semi vowels are termed voiced घोष वर्ण । This means that a background sound is produced from the tremor in the vocal cords in addition to the active sound produced in speaking. The 3rd, 4th and 5th letters of the row class consonants are also घोष वर्ण ।

The 1st and 2nd letters of the row class consonants, the sibilants and the aspirate are termed अघोष वर्ण । This means that no background sound arises from the tremor in the vocal cords.

All row consonants are termed स्पर्श वर्ण Tongue makes contact

http://rachelsenglish.com/ending-voiced-vs-unvoiced-consonants/

The unit of time for enunication is a short vowel, having 1 matra.
The long vowels and diphthongs have 2 matras.
A consonant has only ½ matra and it is supplied with a vowel for proper enunciation.

VOWELS स्वर

Long Vowels are sounded twice as long as the short vowels.

DIPHTHONGS सन्ध्यक्षर (सन्धि – अक्षर) Are combinations of two vowels and are sounded long.

GUTTURALS कण्ठ्य (also known as VELAR)

Sounded from the throat with the tongue resting.

PALATALS तालव्य

Sounded with the tongue raised slightly.

CEREBRALS मूर्धन्य (also known as RETROFLEX or LINGUAL)

Sounded with the tongue touching the roof of the mouth.

DENTALS दन्त्य

Sounded with the tongue distinctly touching the teeth.

LABIALS ओष्ठ्य

Sounded with the lips distinctly touching each other.

Letter Names

The question arises if there are names for letters? Yes there are. A common practise is to attach कार to a letter and that becomes its name.

The vowel अ is called अकार
The vowel आ is called आकार
The vowel इ is called इकार , etc.

The consonant क is called ककार
The consonant ख is called खकार
The consonant ग is called गकार , etc.

There is also a name for all vowels put together. It is अच्
There is also a name for all consonants put together. It is हल्

Then there is the name वर्ग for the 25 row class consonants.
The first row beginning with क् and comprising of the letters क् ख् ग् घ् ङ् is named कवर्ग or simply कु (कुँ=क् उँ,where उँ is a discardable tag)
The second row beginning with च् and comprising of the letters च् छ् ज् झ् is named चवर्ग or simply चु (चुँ) ।
The third row beginning with ट् and comprising of the letters ट् ठ् ड् ढ् ण् is named टवर्ग or simply टु (टुँ) ।
The fourth row beginning with त् and comprising of the letters त् थ् द् ध् न् is named तवर्ग or simply तु (तुँ) ।
The fifth row beginning with प् and comprising of the letters प् फ् ब् भ् म् is named पवर्ग or simply पु (पुँ) ।

There is a special name for र् । It is commonly called the Repha.

Ayogavaha

The Ayogavāha class of characters do not exist independently, but are born in the case of specific combinations of letters in a sentence. Ayogavāha sounds are Candrabindu, Anusvāra, Visarga, Ardha Visarga(Jihvāmūlīya and Upadhmānīya), Nāsikya, Yama and Svarabhakti. These cannot be pronounced independently but depend on a vowel, e.g. अ to be enunciated. Hence named अ–योग–वाह A-yoga-vaha = in flowing union with "A".

CANDRABINDU ँ and ANUSVĀRA ं

Sounds can be produced from the mouth, from the mouth with emphasis on the nose anunāsika, and from the nose alone with the mouth shut. *The term* **nasalization** *is employed to denote that emphasis is on the nose, whereas* **nasal** *means use of nose alone.*

Candrabindu indicates that a vowel is to be pronounced as nasalized. It can also indicate the nasalization of the consonants य्, ल् and व् । Thus the mouth and nose both are employed in sounding the chandrabindu.

Anusvāra is a character that denotes the pure nasal. Thus it is slightly different than the म् which is an anunāsika. Technically it should be pronounced with the mouth shut. It is doable for those who learnt it in their childhood. Most of us pronounce it like the म् in which the lips touch and then open. The anusvāra represents the nasal of the type of letter it precedes; e.g. गंगा = गङ्गा = *gaṅga (river Ganges)*. Refer Ashtadhyayi of Panini 8.3.4 अनुनासिकात् परोऽनुस्वारः appearance of anusvara.

VISARGA ः

Pronounced like *huh* with a soft release of breath. During reading, the visarga takes on the addition of its preceding vowel. Thus utter रामः as ramaha, हरिः as harihi, विष्णुः as vishnuhu.

ARDHA VISARGA ᳵ (Vedic texts only) JIHVAMULIYA, UPADHMANIYA

The visarga becomes an ardha visarga in specific sandhi situations. If it is facing a क or ख , the visarga is called an ardha visarga named Jihvāmūlīya and is written as ᳵ or **X**. If it is facing a प or फ , the visarga is called an ardha visarga named Upadhmānīya and is written as ᳵ or ᳶ. In some earlier texts ᳶ denotes upadhmaniya.

NĀSIKYA हुँ (Vedic texts only) नासिक्य

This nasikya sound is popular in Art of Living programs, however the grammatical connotation is different.

YAMA ᳲ ङ्ँ (sounded like गुँ , गं् Vedic texts only) कुँ खुँ गुँ घुँ - यम

Means addition of a consonant between a consonant and a nasal during Vedic chanting. कुँ is an abbreviation for the initial row consonant letters of each of the five rows viz. क् च् ट् त् प् । कुँ = क् उँ where उँ is a meta tag letter. Characters ꣳ ᳲ represent accentuated anusvāra preceding र , श ष स , ह । The ꣳ supposedly follows short vowels, and ᳲ follows long vowels in the Rudra Puja chanting of the South Indian Krishna Yajur Veda tradition. Some grammarians are of the viewpoint that the yama sound ᳲ indicates the nasalization in particular sandhi cases when the following letter is a sibilant or a repha. In the Rudrashtadhyayi chanting followed in the North Indian tradition, the ज gets accented as य (termed heavy य) in some cases, while ष and gets enunciated as ख ।

SVARABHAKTI (anaptyxis) र् , ल् (स्वर भक्ति)

Means addition of a vowel between two consonants to aid enunciation. A vowel sound akin to ऋ ऌ inserted between र or ल and a following consonant. This sound is supposed to last for a quarter matra मात्रा called अणु । Sound that is half time period of अणु is termed परमाणु ।

Letters that Look similar

क 11	ख 12	ग 13	घ 14	ङ 15
च 21	छ 22	ज 23	झ 24	ञ 25
ट 31	ठ 32	ड 33	ढ 34	ण 35
त 41	थ 42	द 43	ध 44	न 45
प 51	फ 52	ब 53	भ 54	म 55
य र ल व		श ष स ह		

12 ख रव (र adjacent to व in a word)

14 घ ध 44

15 ङ ड 33

23 ज ञ 25

34 ढ द 43

54 भ म 55

Letters that Sound similar

क 11	ख 12	ग 13	घ 14	ङ 15
च 21	छ 22	ज 23	झ 24	ञ 25
ट 31	ठ 32	ड 33	ढ 34	ण 35
त 41	थ 42	द 43	ध 44	न 45
प 51	फ 52	ब 53	भ 54	म 55
य र ल व		श ष स ह		

15 ङ ञ 25

35 ण न 45

33 ड ढ 34

श ष

Conjuncts

Famous conjuncts क्ष , ज्ञ , श्र

क्ष = क् ष , ज्ञ = ज् ञ , श्र = श् र

Common conjuncts त्र , त्त , क्त , द्य , ह्म ,

त्र = त् र , त्त = त् त , क्त = क् त , द्य = द् य , ह्म = ह् म

Repha conjuncts
A preceding repha goes on the top like a hook.

र्क = र् क , र्प = र् प

A following repha is written like a forward slanting slash.

क्र = क् र , प्र = प् र

However in these conjuncts a following repha is like a circumflex.

ट्र = ट् र , ठ्र , ड्र , ढ्र , छ्र , ल्र

Punctuation marks

Sanskrit text whether prose or poetry has a minimum of punctuations. The only visible ones are

AVAGRAHA ऽ

Marks the elision of initial अ due to sandhi.

Double AVAGRAHA ऽऽ

Marks the elision of initial आ due to sandhi.

DANDA also known as VIRAMA

। marks the end of a sentence.

॥ marks the end of a paragraph.

In the case of poetry, a single virama signifies a pause in reading or a half-verse. A double virama means a complete verse.

Abbreviation ॰

A small circle signifies a shortened word or verse.

Some other punctuations are in the form of regular letters.

च means the conjunction "and"

which is also commonly employed as a comma. So we may write *Time, Space, Air, Water and Matter* in Sanskrit as काल खम् वायु जलम् वस्तु च ।

इति means the preposition "thus"

which is also commonly employed as quotation marks. *He said "Shiva is Beautiful"* = शिवम् सुन्दरं इति सः उवाच ।

किम् means the question "what"

which is also commonly employed as a question mark. *What is your name?* is written as भवतः नाम किम् ।

हे means hailing someone "hey"

which is also commonly employed as an exclamation! Hey Ram! is written as हे राम ।

Vowel Matras

A vowel follow a consonant and gets joined to it. A consonant without a vowel will have the presence of halant ◌् e.g. क् ।
Whereas letters having a vowel will not have the halant e.g. क ।

अ when joined to क् becomes क and so on.
आ when joined to क् becomes का and so on. ◌ा
इ when joined to क् becomes कि and so on. ि◌
ई when joined to क् becomes की and so on. ◌ी
उ when joined to क् becomes कु and so on. ◌ु
ऊ when joined to क् becomes कू and so on. ◌ू
ऋ when joined to क् becomes कृ and so on. ◌ृ
ॠ when joined to क् becomes कॄ and so on. ◌ॄ
ऌ when joined to क् becomes कॢ and so on. ◌ॢ
ए when joined to क् becomes के and so on. ◌े
ऐ when joined to क् becomes कै and so on. ◌ै
ओ when joined to क् becomes को and so on. ◌ो
औ when joined to क् becomes कौ and so on. ◌ौ

Anusvara ◌ं joins to a vowel to give अं , कं , किं , कुं etc.

Visarga ◌ः joins to a vowel to give अः , कः , किः , कुः etc.

र् Repha with उ , ऊ is different because it goes in the middle

रु , रू

Writing Matras

Vowel matras मात्रा are written after the letter, above the letter, or below the letter.

◌ा in all cases and the special case of र् उ and र् ऊ
After the letter e.g. आ , रु , रू

◌ि ◌ी , ◌े ◌ै , ◌ो ◌ौ
Above the letter e.g. कि , खी , गे , सै , चो , जौ ,

◌ु ◌ू , ◌ृ ◌ॄ , ◌ॢ
Below the letter e.g. पु , फू , वृ , कॄ , कॢ ,

Some more markings

◌्
To specify a half-letter the halant is added below e.g. ट् , ड् , य् , ब्

◌ँ ◌ं
To specify Nasalization, Candrabindu or Anusvara is added above e.g. माँ , नं

◌ः
To specify aspiration, Visarga is added after e.g. मः , तिः , नुः

Similarly for conjuncts

ध्मा, च्छ्रे , न्यू , न्तिः , क्रू

Alphabet table for letter “k”

Sanskrit alphabet written using the letter क

Mātrās

क का कि की कु कू के कै को कौ कं कः

कृ कॄ कॢ

Accents

क क॒ क॑ क᳚   का का॒ का॑ का᳚   कि कि॒ कि॑ कि᳚   की की॒ की॑ की᳚

कु कु॒ कु॑ कु᳚   कू कू॒ कू॑ कू᳚   के के॒ के॑ के᳚   कै कै॒ कै॑ कै᳚

को को॒ को॑ को᳚   कौ कौ॒ कौ॑ कौ᳚

Nasalization

कँ काँ किँ कीँ कुँ कूँ केँ कैँ कोँ कौँ

Pluta

क३ का३ कि३ की३ कु३ कू३ के३ कै३ को३ कौ३

Ayogavahas occur on specific combinations of letters

मामकाᳵ पाण्डवाश्चैव   त्र्य॑म्बकयँ॑यजामहे   हि॑ꣳसीः   अही॑ꣴश्च   द्विप॑दा॒ याश्

Vedic and Classical Sanskrit

वैदिक तथा लौकिक संस्कृत

Vedic texts such as the Taittiriya Upanishad Shiksha Valli, the Paniniya Shiksha and the Taittiriya Pratisakhya give detailed enumeration of sounds and letters in grammar.

All of these sounds and letters got mingled and reused in various languages around the globe as man journeyed, explored and met peoples from various lands. Some of the vedic sounds are still used in languages such as English, French, Spanish, Tamil, Greek, Latin, Hittite, Russian, Hebrew, Chinese, Japanese, Arabic, Urdu, German, Hindi, Marathi, Nepali while classical Sanskrit has retired them.

Conversely, these languages have had an influence on Sanskrit so its forms in Hindi, Marathi, Nepali have some extra characters that seem to be absent in classical Sanskrit.

Letters ळ and ळ्ह

अग्निमीळे पुरोहितं यज्ञस्य देवमृत्विजम्। Rigveda 1.1.1.1

अग्ने मृळीकं वरुणे सचा विदो मरुत्सु विश्वभानुषु। Rigveda 4.1.1.3

दृळ्हं नरो वचसा दैव्येन व्रजं गोमन्तमुशिजो वि वव्रुः । Rigveda 4.1.1.15

This letter ळ is frequent in Marathi but rare in Hindi. Present day Sanskrit does not use it.

Accents Udata, Anudata _ , Svarita ॑ , Dirgha Svarita ᳚

Ayogavaha Sounds ArdhaVisarga, Yama, Nasikya, Svarabhakti

In the chanting of Rudrashtadhyayi North Indian tradition the sound य (a palatal) is pronounced as ज (a palatal) in particular instances. Written in the text as य ।

Also in some sandhi situations the sound ष (a retroflex) is uttered as ख (a guttural). This is seen in the Shukla Yajurved Madhyandini Samhita. (Rudrashtadhyayi chanting North Indian tradition). Here when ष is followed by a consonant it is uttered as ख , except when ष is followed by the retroflex consonants ट ठ ड ढ ण then it is uttered as ष ।

Nukta

The nukta is a dot placed below-left of a letter. It finds use in Hindi for special enunciation of some words and is also due to the influence of Arabic and Urdu.

क़ ख़ ग़ ज़ ड़ ढ़ फ़ य़

Nukta is not seen in Sanskrit.

Anusvara and Candrabindu usage varies in each language that use the Devanagari script.

Vedic Accents

स्वरः Udata, Anudata, Svarita, Dirgha Svarita

Accents are marks on the vowels that change the pitch. Accents are used to highlight that a particular vowel is to be pronounced in a different pitch. Vary the frequency, vary the tone so that the chanting is noticed by the listener appropriately. These are given in the text by various marks under or on the vowel.

A syllable may be pronounced
from the belly, Anudāta, by dropping the neck slightly = low pitch
from the heart, Udāta, by keeping a straight face = normal pitch
from the forehead, Svarita, by raising the neck slightly = high pitch
elongating the time of enunciation, dīrgha Svarita = high to normal

अनुदात्त Anudāta, underline for a vowel, signifies that the pitch is to be lowered, i.e. the sound should come from the belly.

अन् + उदात्तः = अनुदात्तः = ॒

उदात्त Udāta – The normal chant, keeping a straight face. There is no marking for उदात्तः । When Anudāta is followed by Udāta, or vice versa, then a change in pitch will be noticeable.

Svarita – Raise in pitch by lifting the head slightly.

स्वरितः = ॑ a vertical bar on the vowel

Dīrgha Svarita – raising the pitch for a longer duration

दीर्घ स्वरितः = two vertical bars on the vowel – During chanting, it is noticeable by pronouncing the vowel, giving a short gap, then again pronouncing the vowel.

Listen to vedic chants to notice how the change in pitch works.
https://www.youtube.com/watch?v=vQjBQJqi0Ak Rudram Challakere Brothers
https://www.youtube.com/watch?v=clb22c3QiGc Havan with Rudrashtadhyayi - Vedic fire ritual

Early Scripts and Languages

The Brahmi, Nagari, Gupta, Sharada scripts were used to write the Pali, Prakrit, Magadhi and Sanskrit languages that flourished in India and South East Asia.

Early inscriptions in the Brahmi script date from the times of Emperor Ashoka circa 250 BC.

The Grantha is a historical script that was used to write Sanskrit in Tamil Nadu. Its use gradually declined over the last century and gave way to Devanagari for Sanskrit texts.

https://en.wikipedia.org/wiki/Brahmi_script Brahmi wikipedia
http://www.virtualvinodh.com/ Vinodh Rajan's blog on scripts

Languages that use Devanagari Script

Devanagari is a descendant of the Brahmi script that was used in India a thousand years ago. Currently over a hundred languages use the Devanagari script. Some of these languages are
Assamese or Bodo
Hindi
Konkani
Marathi
Nepali

The Devanagari script is known as *abugida*. Abugida means a form of writing in which the vowels get joined to consonants in a syllable and are treated as a single unit. Such writing is typical of scripts from South Asia.

A Complete Character Set

For typing in Devanagari to be versatile, the following characters need to be present at the minimum in a font set.

Standard set

Standard set with ability to type half-forms of letters e.g. श् ग् च्

Standard set with ability to type conjuncts e.g. ञ्ह ह्ल ष्ट्व ल्ल न्स्म ङ्क

Standard set with ability to type standalone characters

Candrabindu, Anusvara, Visarga, Virama for special use

Extended Vedic set

for accents and ayogavaha sounds and nasalization

for enunciating य in specific cases = य

for characters ळ , ळ्ह

Hindi-Marathi-Nepali-Bihari-Kashmiri set

for nukta as in Hindi ज़, letter ळ for Marathi, etc.

Backward compatibility set

for letters that have changed shape over time in texts

e.g. अ to अ, झ to झ, क्ष for क्ष , ण to ण , क्ष to क्ष

Punctuation set for virama, danda, etc.

Special characters set - for rupee symbol ₹ , square root √ for displaying the dhatus, etc.

Roman transliteration set – English letters with diacritical marks

e.g. iso 15919 letters ñ ṅ ṇ

Correct spacing, height, width for matras and accents and diacritics

The Unicode Standard 9.0 allots the range

0900 – 097F for Devanagari

A8E0 – A8FF for Devanagari extended

1CD0 – 1CFF for Vedic Extensions

http://www.unicode.org/charts/

http://software.sil.org/gentium/support/character-set-support/

Standard set

अ आ इ ई उ ऊ ऋ ॠ ऌ ॡ   ए ऐ ओ औ   अं अः

क	ख	ग	घ	ङ
च	छ	ज	झ	ञ
ट	ठ	ड	ढ	ण
त	थ	द	ध	न
प	फ	ब	भ	म

य र ल व

श ष स   ह

० १ २ ३ ४ ५ ६ ७ ८ ९

Standard set with Half-forms of consonants

क क्	ख ख्	ग ग्	घ घ्	ङ
च च्	छ छ्	ज ज्	झ झ्	ञ ञ्
ट	ठ	ड	ढ	ण ण्
त त्	थ थ्	द	ध ध्	न न्
प प्	फ फ्	ब ब्	भ भ्	म म्
य य् र ल ल् व व्				
श श् श् ष ष् स स् ह ह्				

Matras, nukta, nasalization, accents, diacritics

◌ँ   ◌ं ˙   ◌ः :   ◌् ˎ   ऽ   ॐ   य   ₹

◌ा ा◌   ि◌ ◌ी   ◌ु ◌ू   ◌ृ ◌ॄ   ◌ॢ ^   क़   ख़   ग़

◌े ◌ै   ◌ो ◌ौ   _   ˈ ॥   ◌़   ज़   ड़   ढ़

फ़   य़   ᳵ ᳶ   ᳩ   °   । ॥   ꣳ ꣴ   √

अ   झ   ण   ल   ∞   ळ   ऴ

Ḍ   ḍ   Ḥ   ḥ   Ḷ   ḷ   Ṁ   ṁ

Ṃ   ṃ   Ṅ   ṅ   Ṇ   ṇ   Ṛ   ṛ

Ṟ   ṟ   Ṡ   ṡ   Ṣ   ṣ   Ṭ   ṭ

For beautiful typesetting, the following characters should be properly spaced in a Devanagari font.

The vedic accent anudata below a vowel

e.g. कु॒ rather than कु॒ or कु॒

The vedic accent svarita above a vowel

e.g. की॑ rather than की॑

The vedic accent double svarita above a vowel

e.g. की᳚ rather than की᳚

Written versus Spoken

Sanskrit words in a sentence coalesce due to conjuncts, sandhis or compounding. Hence written Sanskrit is ***slightly different*** than spoken Sanskrit. As such a teacher is required for one to learn how to read the scriptures or vedic texts, especially the Bhagavad Gita and the Rudra Puja.

https://www.zorbabooks.com/store/religion/bhagavad-gita-for-chanting/ Bhagavad Gita for Chanting

https://www.zorbabooks.com/store/religion/rudra-puja/ Rudra Puja

https://www.amazon.com/dp/B0718W5ZQF Bhagavad Gita Reader - All verses in 4 quarters

Avagraha Ayogavaha Visarga Anusvara

Reading or chanting a Sanskrit text takes into account the appearance of Ayogavaha characters. These characters are uttered in a specific way, that is usually taught in a gurukul system.

Even though traditionally the ayogavaha characters are only specified in the Vedic texts, by definition we can include them to mean the Visarga and the Anusvara.

अवग्रह Avagraha ऽ is not to be chanted, i.e. it is a silent letter.

It signifies that an अ has been dropped due to sandhi.

e.g. Recite प्रथमोऽध्यायः as प्रथमोध्यायः ,

verse 2.14 आगमापयिनोऽनित्याः as आगमापयिनोनित्याः , etc.

विसर्ग Visarga ःः is pronounced variously, a brief mention

A visarga is pronounced aspirated ह् followed by the sound of the preceding vowel. Thus नमः is to be chanted as नम ह

verse 2.41 बुद्धिः is to be chanted as बुद्धि हि

verse 2.43 स्वर्गपराः is to be chanted as स्वर्गपरा हा

verse 2.47 कर्मफलहेतुर्भूः is to be chanted as कर्मफलहेतुर्भू हू

This rule is valid only when a visarga is at the end, i.e. a virama is present. This rule also applies when a visarga is followed by a pause, as at a quarter verse.

However, a visarga in close proximity with another letter gets replaced with another letter or even gets dropped. This is reflected in this book by substituting the changed letter. (popular editions of the Gita show the visarga rather than the actual letter that is to be chanted). E.g.

Visarga when followed by श or च is pronounced as श्

तेजः क्षमा धृतिः शौचम् , अद्रोहो नातिमानिता । तेजश् क्षमा धृतिश् शौचम्

भवन्ति सम्पदं दैवीम् , अभिजातस्य भारत ॥ १६.३

Visarga when followed by स or त is pronounced as स्

कार्यकरणकर्तृत्वे ,   हेतुः प्रकृतिरुच्यते ।

पुरुषः सुखदुःखानाम् , भोक्तृत्वे हेतुरुच्यते ॥ १३.२० पुरुषस् सुखदुःखानाम्

Visarga when followed by vowel or soft consonant is dropped or changes to ओ as per context. Consider verse 2.16 नासतः विद्यते भावः नाभावः विद्यते सतः । and as it appears in popular editions नासतो विद्यते भावो नाभावो विद्यते सतः । because the visarga has been changed to ओ due to sandhi. And here in this book, due to the pause in chanting नासतो विद्यते भावः ,   नाभावो विद्यते सतः । the visarga is shown because भावो is to be chanted as भावः i.e. as भाव ह ।

Similarly

पिताहमस्य जगतः ,   माता धाता पितामहः ।

वेद्यं पवित्रमोङ्कारः ,   ऋक्साम यजुरेव च ॥ ९.१७

येऽप्यन्यदेवता भक्ताः ,   यजन्ते श्रद्धयान्विताः ।

तेऽपि मामेव कौन्तेय ,   यजन्त्यविधिपूर्वकम् ॥ ९.२३

Also, a visarga changes to a repha in certain instances, or gets dropped in other cases.

Ardha Visarga ᳵ जिह्वामूलीय / उपधमानीय

Optionally, a visarga ः becomes an ardha visarga when the following letter is a क or ख and is called jihvamuliya. When the following letter is प or फ it is called upadhmaniya. But it remains a visarga when the following letter is क्ष (क्-ष).

Visarga preceding क, ख is pronounced aspirated ह्

बुद्धियुक्तो जहातीह ,   उभे सुकृतदुष्कृते ।

तस्माद् योगाय युज्यस्व ,   योगᳵ कर्मसु कौशलम् ॥ २.५०

Visarga preceding प, फ is pronounced aspirated फ़

धर्मक्षेत्रे कुरुक्षेत्रे , समवेता युयुत्सवः ।

मामकाᳶ पाण्डवाश्चैव , किम् अकुर्वत सञ्जय ॥ १.१

Notice that generally a visarga is at the end of a word, but in rare cases it comes within a word (verse 13.20 सुखदुःखानाम् , verse 18.3 यज्ञदानतपᳵकर्म).

Anusvara ं is pronounced as nasalized म् ।

However Sandhi grammar rules state that Anusvara changes to a corresponding nasal when followed by a class consonant, *albeit optionally*. Very few pandits make the Anusvara sound as ङ् when followed by ग, as ञ् when followed by च or as न् when followed by त् / द् ।

पश्यैतां पाण्डुपुत्राणाम् , आचार्य महतीं चमूम् । महतीञ् चमूम्

व्यूढां द्रुपदपुत्रेण , तव शिष्येण धीमता ॥ १.३ व्यूढान् द्रुपदपुत्रेण

Others chant an Anusvara as यँ् when followed by य ।

कर्म ब्रह्मोद्भवं विद्धि , ब्रह्माक्षरसमुद्भवम् ।

तस्मात् सर्वगतं ब्रह्म , नित्यं यज्ञे प्रतिष्ठितम् ॥ ३.१५ नित्यँ् यज्ञे

In any case it is ok if Anusvara is pronounced as म् ।

Specific Conjuncts

ह्न , ह्ण , ह्म These conjuncts are chanted as नः , णः , मः resp.

पवन⊠ पवतामस्मि , रामः शस्त्रभृतामहम् ।

झषाणां मकरश्चास्मि , स्रोतसामस्मि जाह्नवी ॥ १०.३१ जानःवी

i.e. though it is ह् न , pronunciation is न ह । These letters are chanted with emphasis on the chest.

स्फोटन Sphotana

When a व्यञ्जन is followed by a क or क्ष there is a natural pause in reading aloud.

Modern Editors

How to type in Sanskrit?

A standard method to insert any symbol is to look up its code in the Unicode Chart. Then type that code and press **ALT+X** keys.
e.g. to insert the rupee symbol, type its code 20B9. Pressing **ALT+X** keys converts it to ₹ i.e. type 20B9**ALT+X**
e.g. to type the Om symbol, type its code 0950. Pressing **ALT+X** keys converts it to ॐ i.e. type 0950**ALT+X**

Unicode charts are available at http://www.unicode.org/charts/

However this method will prove cumbersome to type a page or continuous text in Sanskrit. So the proper way is to ***enable the Sanskrit or Hindi keyboard*** in Windows or Mac or the smartphone.

OpenOffice, MS Word, Adobe Pagemaker and Indesign, and Tex are the standard word processors.
https://www.openoffice.org/
https://products.office.com/en-in/word
http://www.adobe.com/in/products/indesign.html
https://www.tug.org/
https://www.ctan.org/tex-archive/language/devanagari/velthuis/?lang=en

Additional writers with support for typing in Indian languages are
http://software.nhm.in/products/writer
http://www.lipikaar.com/
http://www.lexilogos.com/keyboard/sanskrit_devanagari.htm
http://www.baraha.com/

Fonts

Some good unicode compliant Devanagari fonts are
Sanskrit 2003
https://omkarananda-ashram.org/Sanskrit/itranslator2003.htm

Siddhanta
http://svayambhava.blogspot.in/

Annapurna SIL
http://software.sil.org/annapurna/

from CDAC
https://cdac.in/index.aspx?id=dl_mlingual_tools

And some excellent legacy Devanagari fonts are
New Delhi, Kruti Dev, Chanakya, Shusha

Keyboard Mapping for Phonetic Typing

http://www.mywhatever.com/sanskrit/vidyut/index.html

https://ubcsanskrit.ca/keyboards.html

Processing Tools

http://sanskritdocuments.org/processing_tools/processing_tools.html

Devanagari Typesetting

Basic Requirements and a typical method

1. a software like MS **Word** or LaTex
2. preferably a unicode compliant font like **Sanskrit 2003**
3. print to pdf printer like **pdfCreator** http://www.pdfforge.org/pdfcreator
4. Enabling the **Sanskrit keyboard** in control panel - Regional & Language settings
5. After the document has been typed in Devanagari, one must print it to pdfCreator with the save setting **pdf/X**. This **embeds** all the fonts and the resulting pdf file can be easily rendered correctly on any machine, operating system, or device.

Transliteration Standards

Sanskrit words are written using Devanagari script. An English speaking person who is used to Roman script can use the transcribing facility to read Sanskrit. There are different conventions to transcribe Devanagari to Roman script.

1. IAST
2. Hunterian system
3. National Library at Kolkata romanization
4. ISO 15919
5. Harvard-Kyoto
6. ITRANS scheme
7. Velthuis
8. SLP1

https://en.wikipedia.org/wiki/Devanagari_transliteration

Devanagari Transliteration Tool
https://www.ashtangayoga.info/sanskrit/

The ISO 15919 standard
http://www.iso.org/iso/iso_catalogue/catalogue_tc/catalogue_detail.htm?csnumber=28333

Devanagari Latin ISO 15919 Chart

a	ā	i	ī	u	ū	r̥	r̥̄	l̥	
अ	आ	इ	ई	उ	ऊ	ऋ	ॠ	ऌ	
						◌ृ	◌ॄ	◌ॢ	
ē	ai	ō	au	ṁ	m̐	ḥ	Ardha visarga		
ए	ऐ	ओ	औ	◌ं	◌ँ	◌ः	ᳲ		
Consonants are shown with a vowel a=अ for uttering									
ka	क	ca	च	ṭa	ट	ta	त	pa	प
kha	ख	cha	छ	ṭha	ठ	tha	थ	pha	फ
ga	ग	ja	ज	ḍa	ड	da	द	ba	ब
gha	घ	jha	झ	ḍha	ढ	dha	ध	bha	भ
ṅa	ङ	ña	ञ	ṇa	ण	na	न	ma	म
ya	ra	la	va		ḷa	ʻ			
य	र	ल	व		ळ	ऽ			
					Consonant only				
śa	ṣa	sa	ha		**ka**	क्अ = क			
श	ष	स	ह		**k**	क्			

Note – halant ◌् is not a separate character in the transliteration. It simply means lack of vowel in the consonant. e.g. Both these words end in "n" but one has a halant in Devanagari. So the word without the halant has a vowel added to it in transliteration. E.g. Both these words end in "n" but one has a halant in Devanagari. So the word without the halant has a vowel added to it in transliteration.

Arju**na** अर्जुन śrī bhagavā**n** श्री भगवान्

Sanskrit Schools

Samskrita Bharati is a premier organisation that teaches Sanskrit.

http://www.vasmp.org/ Veda Agama Samskrutha Maha Pathshala
http://www.sanskrit.nic.in/ Rashtriya Sanskrit Sansthan
https://www.samskritabharati.in/ Samskrita Bharati
http://avg-sanskrit.org/ Arsha Vijnana Gurukulam
https://www.madrassanskritcollege.edu.in/
Madras Sanskrit College

https://www.chinfo.org/index.php/easy-sanskrit-course
Chinmaya Mission

http://www.rkmath.org/courses-and-syllabuses-sanskrit.aspx?pid=237
Ramakrishan Math

https://www.youtube.com/watch?v=KnIBwHJPWuA
Sanskrit Language teaching through Video
https://www.youtube.com/watch?v=9EiyBDWITcA
Spoken Sanskrit Series

http://www.columbia.edu/cu/mesaas/languages/sanskrit/
Columbia University, New York
https://www.brown.edu/academics/classics/sanskrit-studies-brown
Brown University, Rhode Island

http://www.sai.uni-heidelberg.de/abt/IND/en/links/links.php?sanskrit_studies
University of Heidelberg, Germany
https://www.bun.kyoto-u.ac.jp/en/ Kyoto University, Japan
http://www.americansanskrit.com/ American Sanskrit Institute
https://sas.fas.harvard.edu/sanskrit Harvard University
http://web.mit.edu/samskritam/www/ MIT Students

Sanskrit Book Publishers

Motilal Banarsidass, Gita Press and Samskrita Bharati are popular.

https://www.samskritabharati.in/bookstore
https://www.mlbd.com/
http://www.gitapress.org/
http://www.chowkhambasanskritseries.com/
http://chaukhambabooks.in/index.php
http://www.rkmkhar.org/ideas/bookshop/
https://www.giri.in/giri-books
http://vedah.com/
http://www.mrmlonline.com/
http://www.parimalpublication.com/

Vedanta Book House in Chamrajpet, Bangalore has a good collection of Sanskrit books from various publishers.

Sanskrit Scholars

Mataji Swamini Brahmaprakasananda Saraswati, Nagpur
http://www.arshavijnanagurukulamnagpur.org/

Pushpa Dikshit, Bilaspur
http://www.pushpadikshit.com/

A.S Sundara Murthy Sivam, Bangalore
http://www.vasmp.org/

Janardana Hegde, Bangalore
https://samskritabharati.in/

George Cardona, USA
https://www.ling.upenn.edu/people/cardona

Madhav M. Deshpande, USA
https://lsa.umich.edu/asian/people/faculty/mmdesh.html

Saroja Bhate, Pune
http://www.unipune.ac.in/dept/fine_arts/sanskrit_and_pakrit/sanpak_webfiles/profile.htm

Ulrich Stiehl, Germany
http://www.sanskritweb.net/

Gary Tubb, USA
http://salc.uchicago.edu/faculty/tubb

A Sanskrit Speaking Town

Mattur in Shimoga district of Karnataka is a hamlet famous for the fact that the avaerage resident speaks Sanskrit. Its twin town Hosahalli does too.

Some other places are Ganoda hamlet in Banswara district of Rajasthan, Jhiri in Rajgarh district of Madhya Pradesh, Mohad in Narsinhpur district of Madhya Pradesh, Shyamsundarpur in Kendujhar district of Orissa, Bhantoli in Rudraprayag district of Uttarakhand.

https://en.wikipedia.org/wiki/Mattur

https://www.youtube.com/watch?v=s0I8h5oCbrQ

http://thelandoutthere.com/the-last-existing-sanskrit-village-mathur-karnataka/

http://globalvarnasramamission.blogspot.in/2012/01/five-indian-villages-where-sanskrit-is.html

https://thammayya.wordpress.com/2008/10/13/sanskrit-speaking-village-in-madhya-pradesh/

https://www.youtube.com/watch?v=lHLIy-WHDew

Glossary

अक्षर – syllable, alphabet, letter, e.g. अ phoneme
अघोष वर्ण – unvoiced consonant e.g. क, ख, श, ष , स, ह
अणु – ¼ मात्रा काल Enunciated for a length of a quarter matra time period.
अनुदात्त – low pitch
अनुनासिका – Anunāsikā i.e. Nasalized, mouth along with nose
अनुस्वार – ◌ं Anusvāra अं
अन्तःस्थ – य् र् ल् व् the semivowel letters, also known as **liquid** letters, letters intermediate between vowels and consonants
अयोगवाह – ◌ँ ◌ं ◌ः ᳵ ꣳ ꣲ ꣴ candrabindu, Anusvāra, Visarga, Ardha Visarga, Jihvāmūlīya, Upadhmānīya, Yama, Nāsikya, Svarabhakti. A dependent letter arising out of vowel sandhi.
अवग्रह – ऽ Avagraha, indicates elision of the vowel अ or आ
उच्चारण – Enunciation
उदात्त – normal pitch
ऊष्म – श् ष् स् the sibilant letters, also called **spirants** or **fricatives.** The hissing sounds.
ऋग्वेद प्रातिशाख्य – Rigved Pratisakhya, a text dealing with letters and phonetics
गुरु स्वर – a syllable of two or more matras, e.g. long vowel आ, conjunct consonant श्च
घोष वर्ण – voiced
तैत्तिरीय प्रातिशाख्य – Taittiriya Pratisakhya, a text dealing with letters and phonetics
दीर्घ – आ ई ऊ ॠ ए ऐ ओ औ long vowels and syllables, e.g. का, के Take double the time of speaking compared to the short vowels.
नासिक्य – हुँ / हूँ sound. An ayogavaha

परमाणु – 1/8 मात्रा काल Time period half of Aṇu
पाणिनीय शिक्षा – Paniniya Siksha, a text dealing with alphabets and phonetics
प्रातिशाख्य – Pratisakhya is an ancient text dealing with the letters and phonetics of the Sanskrit language
प्लुत – Pluta vowel. Elongation in time of speaking e.g. अ३ , ई३ etc. Used also when calling someone from a distance.
मात्रा – Time taken to utter a letter. A consonant takes half matra time period, whereas a short vowel takes one matra time period. Also called Mora. Alternate meaning is the vowel symbol.
यम – कुँ, खुँ, गुँ, घुँ sounds. गुँ is written as ॽँ,ङ्ँ Ayogavaha
लघु स्वर – a syllable of one matra, e.g. short vowel अ
वर्ग – row class consonant letters, these are 25
वर्ण – letter of the alphabet
वाजसनेयी प्रातिशाख्य – Vajasneyi Pratisakhya, a text dealing with letters and phonetics
विसर्जनीय – ः Visarga विसर्ग अः
वैदिक – Vedic Sanskrit of the ancient texts
व्यञ्जन – consonant
संयुक्त अक्षर – conjunct consonant, e.g. क्त
सन्ध्यक्षर, सन्धि अक्षर – ए ऐ ओ औ the diphthong vowel letters
स्पर्श वर्ण – contacted letter, a consonant known as a **plosive**
स्फोटन – sphoṭana – when a consonant is followed by a letter of the कवर्ग then a natural gap in enunciation occurs
स्वर – vowel. Also means accent on vowel e.g. Anudata
स्वरित – high pitch
ह्रस्व – अ इ उ ऋ ऌ the short vowels and syllables, e.g. क, कि etc.

References

Author	Title	Year	Ed	Publisher
V S Apte	संस्कृत हिन्दी कोश (1890 Ed)	1997	1st	Oriental Book Center, Delhi
Dr. Somlekha	पाणिनीय शिक्षा	2014	1st	Chaukhamb a Sanskrit Pratishthan, Delhi
Shivraj Acharya Kondinyayan	पाणिनीय शिक्षा	2012	1st	Chaukhamb a Surbharti Prakashan, Varanasi
Yudhisthir Mimamsak	शिक्षा सूत्राणि	2014	1st	Ram Lal Kapoor Trust, Sonipat
Shriram Sharma Acharya	ऋग्वेद संहिता	2005	1st	Yugnirman Yojana, Mathura
Dr. R. L. Kashyap	ऋग्वेद् मन्त्र संहिता Rig Veda Mantra Samhita	2003	1st	Sri Aurobindo Kapali Shastry Institute of Vedic Culture, Bangalore
Manomohan Ghosh	Paniniya Siksa	1938	1st	University of Calcutta, Calcutta
Radheyshyam Khemka	शुक्ल यजुर्वेदीय रुद्राष्टाध्यायी	2016	1st	Gita Press, Gorakhpur
Thomas Egenes	Introduction to Sanskrit - Part Two	2000	1st	Motilal Banarsidass , Delhi
Pushpa Dikshit	अष्टाध्यायी सूत्रपाठः	2010	1st	Samskrita Bharati, New Delhi
Acharya Swami Vijayanand Puri	तैत्तिरीयोपनिषत्	1999	1st	Kailash Ashram, Rishikesh

Rajendralala Mitra	तैत्तिरीयप्रातिशाख्यं त्रिभाष्यरत्ननाम टीकासहितम्	1872	1st	Asiatic Society of Bengal, Calcutta
K. Rangacharya and R. Shama Sastri	तैत्तिरीयप्रातिशाख्यम् सोमयार्यविरचित त्रिभाष्यरत्नाख्य व्याख्यया गार्ग्यगोपालयज्वविरचित वैदिकाभरणाख्य व्याख्यया च सहितम्	1906	1st	Government Oriental Library, Mysore
William D. Whitney	The Taittiriya Pratisakhya with its commentary the Tribhashyaratna (1868 Ed)	1973	1st	Motilal Banarsidass , Delhi
William Dwight Whitney	A Sanskrit Grammar , Including both the classical language, and the older dialects, of veda and brahmana	1879	1st	Leipzig, Breitkopf and Hārtel
C. C. Uhlenbeck	A Manual of Sanskrit Phonetics	1898	1st	Uhlenbeck, London
Charles Wikner	A Practical Sanskrit Introductory	1996	1st	Charles Wikner, South Africa
Ashwini Kumar Aggarwal	Rudra Puja	2016	1st	Zorba Books, Gurgaon

From the Net

http://sanskritdictionary.com/ Sanskrit online dictionary
http://spokensanskrit.de/ Spoken Sanskrit online dictionary
http://www.sanskritsounds.com/ Sanskrit Sounds by Nikolai Bachman
http://www.aa.tufs.ac.jp/~tjun/sktdic/ Apte Sanskrit English - Takashima's Labo
http://www.tilakpyle.com/sanskrit.htm Sanskrit Pronunciation Guide

Audio Learning

Vyoma Linguistics Labs Foundation, Bangalore http://www.vyomalabs.in/

ॐ

Epilogue

The ॐ symbol is created from three parts, namely the "3" shape of अ, the knob from ऊ, and the candrabindu ँ that is used to indicate a nasalized vowel. In other words, Sattva Rajas Tamas, or the Trinity that supports creation.

सर्वे भवन्तु सुखिनः । सर्वे सन्तु निरामयाः ।

सर्वे भद्राणि पश्यन्तु । मा कश्चिद् दुःख भाग् भवेत् ॥

ॐ शान्तिः शान्तिः शान्तिः

When faith has blossomed in life, Every step is led by the Divine.

Sri Sri Ravi Shankar

Om Namah Shivaya

जय गुरुदेव

9 789348 012272

Printed at Repro India Ltd.